MARRIAGES

AT THE REFORMED DUTCH CHURCH

IN JAMAICA, L.I., NY

1803 - 1851

by the pastor

REV. JACOB SCHOONMAKER

Published 2011 by
South Oxford Press
Oxford, NY 13830

Originally Copied by
Josephine C. Frost
(Mrs. Samuel Knapp Frost)
Brooklyn, NY
1913

ISBN-13: 978-1461157809
ISBN-10: 1461157803

South Oxford Press
2139 County Road 3
Oxford, NY 13830
southoxfordpress@live.com
www.southoxfordpress.com

PREFACE

This is a transcribed copy of a book originally published in 1913. Every attempt has been made to prevent errors in the transcription. If the reader finds what they believe are errors, they can email the publisher at the email address on the copyright page.

As time permits, we will be publishing more books with baptismal data from this particular church.

South Oxford Press is a publisher of old, rare, and out-of-print books that are of continuing interest to various segments of the population. Because of personal interests in the subject, we tend to lean heavily towards genealogical books, especially those with historical family records, such as this book contains.

We make a serious effort to transcribe these books from original copies, where available, rather than publishing scanned image copies or optical character read copies, which are highly susceptible to error.

New copies of books that we have published can be found at the web-site listed on the copyright page.

Robert G. Yorks

i

PUBLISHER'S NOTES

Throughout the book, abbreviations appear, both in the names of locations and in the surnames & given names of the marriage parties. To the best of my ability, I will try to clarify those, here.

Locations

F. M./Fos. M.	-	Foster Meadows
G. N.	-	Great Neck
N. T.	-	New Town/Newtown
N. Br.	-	New Bridge
N. U.	-	New Utrecht
O. B.	-	Oyster Bay
Sp./Spr./Spr'd	-	Springfield

Bushwick (northern area of Kings Co.)
Dutch Kills (part of Long Island City/Newtown)
Flatbush (central area of Kings Co.)
Flatlands (eastern area of Kings Co.)
Foster Meadows (part of Hempstead)
Great Neck (part of North Hempstead)
Hudson (maybe south of Albany, NY on the Hudson River)
Manhasset (in Nassau Co. - east of Queens Co.)
New Bridge (part of Hempstead)
New Lebanon (maybe s-east of Albany, along the state line)
New Lots/New Lotts (part of Flatbush)
New Utrecht (western area of Kings Co.)
Oyster Bay (Town east of Hempstead)
Plains (prob. Hempstead Plains)
Springfield (western area of Hempstead)
Success (part of North Hempstead)
Williamsburgh (part of Bushwick)

NAMES of PEOPLE

Some of these abbreviations are obvious, but for completeness, I have tried to include all of them.

Abm.	Abram/Abraham
Alex.	Alexander
And.	Andrew
Aug.	Augustus
Benj.	Benjamin
Cath.	Catherine
Chas.	Charles
Cors.	Cornelius
Danl.	Daniel
Eliz(a)	Elizabeth
Fred.	Frederick
Geo.	George
Hend'k	Hendrick
Jas.	James
Jno./Jona	Jonathan
Jos.	Joseph
Mat.	Matthew
Nathl.	Nathaniel
Nich.	Nicholas
Rich.	Richard
Robt.	Robert
Saml.	Samuel
St.	Stephen
Thos.	Thomas
Tim.	Timothy
V.	Van [eg: Van Dine]

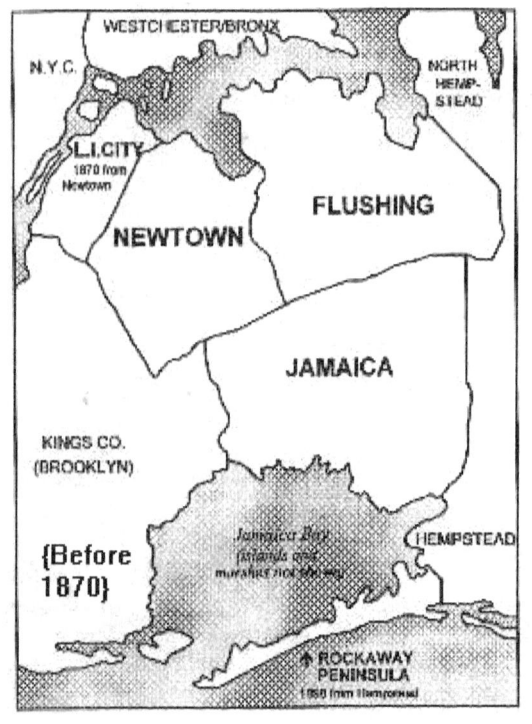

OUTLINE MAP
of
QUEENS COUNTY
(Jamaica, Flushing, Newtown, & LI City)
and
ADJACENT COUNTIES

iv

1803	Feb. 3	Saml. Waldron & Ann Emans
	Dec. 25	Benj. J. Waldron & Rachel Wilmuth
1804	Feb. 2	Garret Stryker & Ann Polhemus
	Mar. 3	Rich. North & Phebe Debois
	"	Wm. Fowler & Mary Lamberson
	Mar. 24	Aury Bennet & Phebe Boerum
	June 4	Saml. Demot & Anna Pearsall
	July 14	Jacobus Hegeman & Eve Debevoise
	Sep. 8	Timothy Nostrand & Tryntie Lott
	Dec. 4	John Bennet & Polly Rhodes
	Dec. 27	Jas. Hendriksen & Caty Oldfield
	Dec. 29	St. Boerum & Rebecca White
1805	Jan. 17	Cors. Eldert & Margaret Ryder
	May 10	Wm. Underhill & Geische Burroughs

1805	May 23	Henry Eldert & Sarah Emans
	June 20	David Miller & Magdalen Boerum
	Aug. ---	Mr. Denard & Widow Polhemus
	Sep. 16	John Lawrence & Eliza Remsen
	Nov. 23	John Snediker & Matchte Monfort
	Dec. 18	Anthony Smith & Jane Remsen
1806	Jan. 17	John Denton & Eliz. Edsely
	Feb. 1	Isaac Rapelye & Peggy Polhemus
	Feb. 4	Aury Remsen & Sally Higbie
	Mar. 15	Andrew Stockholm & Peggy Bragaw
	Apr. 20	John Durlan & Mary Powel
	Apr. 27	Jas. Mackerel & Aletta Fish
	June 11	Thos. H. Betts & Emmy Hoit
	July 30	John Berger & Matie Hendrikson

1806	Oct. 23	John Snediker & Eliz. Eldert
1807	Jan. 14	John Trofford & Grace Rapelye
	Feb. 23	Samuel V. P. Child & Miss Frances W. Jones of city of New York
	Feb. 7	John V. Alst & Aletta Polhemus
	June 21	Abm. Eldert & Eliz. Doughty
	Dec. 1	Theodorus Polhemus & Polly S------?
1808	Feb. 24	Williamson Ryder & Janatie Williamson
	Mar. 9	Peter Stoothoff & Lamatie Bennet
	April 17	Jonas Hall & Miss Hannah A. Mills
	May 29	Cors. Lamberson & Eliza Rowe
	July 17	Bernardus Bennet & Eliz. Mills
	Oct. 3	Thos. Remsen & Polly Remsen
	Oct. 22	David Gardner & Eleanor Willett
	Dec. 15	Edward Tompkins & Eliza. Way

1809	Jan. 1	Benj. Loweree & Priscilla Ireland
	Jan. 5	Jacob Hegeman & Nelly Duryea
	Feb. 2	Derik Lambertson & Altie Remsen
	Feb. 8	John Bennet & Sarah Smith
	Feb. 28	Fred. V. Lew & Hannah Smith
	----	Wynant Bennet & Phebe V. Wicklen
	April 27	Jas. Cortelyou & Anna V. Dine
	May 16	John A. Ditmars & Hannah Wykof
	July 18	John Waters & Agnes Snedeker
	Aug. 13	Abm. Durye & Miss Cozyn
	Dec. 12	Ralph Howard & Betsy Higgins
1810	Jan. 14	Wm. McKee & Eliz. Jones
	Mar. 5	John R. Ludlow & Cotalina Ditmars
	Mar. 10	David Abrams & Charity Antonides

1810	July 16	Abm. Stoothof & Mary Pettit
	July 14	Rev. Abm. Hoffman & -------- Durye
	Aug. 5	Willet Skidmore & Eliz. Johnson
	Aug. 11	John Bolton & Eliza Reed
	Oct. 28	Geo. Snediker & Hannah V. Dine
	Nov. 3	Michael Schoonmaker & Susan Ludlow
	Dec. 7	Jeromus Snedeker & Maria V. Wicklen
1811	Jan. 3	Rich. Spragg & Sarah Way
	Jan. 19	Wm. Tilton & Cath. Ann Penfold
	Mar. 20	Thos. Moore & Sally Luyster
	Mar. 22	John Couwenhoven & Polly Coe
	April 11	Wm. V. Dine & Marva Wykof
	April 28	Benj. Patterson & Hannah Provost
	May 22	Abm. Polhemus & Cornelia Suydam

1811	May 29	Moses Debevois & Miss Mary Durye
	July 7	John Cozyn & Beyst Boerum
	Sep. ---	Michael Fash & Mary Ann Willet
	Oct. 13	Purdy Fowler Harriet Fowler
	Oct. 28	Mr. Stryker & Ann Terhune
	--------	Wm. Johnson & -------? Antonides
	---------	Johanis Selover & Charity Smith
	Oct. 12	Jas. Hyatt & Anna Monfort
	Oct. 12	Thos. K. K. Hyatt & Cath. Monfort
	Aug. 25	John Tompkins & Hannah Springsteen
1812	Jan. 9	Abm. Hegeman & Anna Lott
	Jan. 13	Rem Remsen & Sarah Bennet
	March 23	Wm. I. Brower & Mary Hyatt
	March 31	John Spader & Phebe Lott

1812	June 22	Benj. Moore & Jane Rapelye
	Sep. 4	Rich. Holland & Ellen Leech
	Oct. 31	Wm. T. Smith & Hannah Watkins
	Nov. 17	Nich. V. Arsdale & Rebecca Mills
	Dec. 8	Saml. Higbie & Sarah Hendrikson
	Dec. 15	Wm. Smith & Eleaner Carpenter
	Dec. 19	John Wickes, Jr. & Mary Ann Hendrikson
1814	Jan. 5	John Martin & Sally Brinkerhof
	Jan. 11	Jacob Polhemus & Hannah Townsend
	Jan. 30	Anson Higbie & Susannah Higbie
	Jan. 31	Murray Cassedy & Margaret Holmes
	Feb. 11	Jonas Seaman & Nelly Mott
	Mar. 26	Wm. Rayner & Ida Lane
	April 4	Cors. Ditmars & Ann Debevoise

1814	April 6	Jas. Herriman & Mary Totten
	June 18	Wm. Hegeman & Jas. Springsteen
	July 17	Benj. Denton & Mary Snedeker
	July 23	Saml. Pierson & Sarah Johnson
	Aug. 4	Danl. Lake & Jane Debevoise
	Aug. 25	John Beagle & Hannah Lambertson
	Nov. 1	Hallet Pierson & Patty Hicks
	Dec. 26	Albert Hoogland & Jane Willis
1815	Jan. 1	Jacob Debevois & Catalina Ditmars
	Jan. 10	Cors. Vandeveer & Maria Eldert
	Jan. 29	Howard V. Dine & Abigail Springsteen
	Feb. 17	Rich. Eldert & Phebe Willis
	Feb. 19	Jas. Hendriksen & Eliz. Hegeman
	Feb. 24	John R. Schermerhorn & Jane Howard

1815	Feb. 25	John I. Lott & Jemima Coevert
	Mar. 1	Jas. Morrel & Mary Rennie
	Mar. 9	Luke Eldert & Phebe V. Wicklen
	April 16	Gastavus Baylies & Cath. Bloom
	May 26	Hend'k. Hendrikson & Nauchie Bennet
	July 17	Wm. Deeman & Hannah Haviland
	Aug. 24	Wm. Shepherdson & Susan Polhemus
	Aug. 27	John Sackett & Sally Morrel
	Sep. 18	Isaac Bergen & Sarah Lamberson
	Oct. 15	Thos. Whiting & Phebe Lawrence
	Oct. 25	Simeon Lambertson & Mary Bedell
	Nov. 15	John Higbie & Ruth Hendrikson
	Dec. 6	John Smith & Eliz. Skidmore
	Dec. 17	John Covert & Mary Murray

1816	June 1	Benj. Denton & Eliz. Fabel
	"	Corns. Ditmis & Adriana Debevoise
	June 23	Jas. Strong & Aletta Remsen
	June 29	Jesse Abrams & Phebe Bennet
	-------	Noah Wetmore & Margaret Brower
1817	Feb. 13	David Henson & Maria Rayner
	Feb. 22	St. Williamson & Johanna Cozine
	Mar. 13	Israle C. Holmes & Maria Couwenhoven
	Mar. 29	Eldert Eldert & Maria Ryder
	April 10	Nicholas Wykof & Ann Durye
	May 1	Hend'k Brinkerhof & Phebe Bloom
	May 10	Thos. Hoit & Getty Remsen
	July 3	John Lambertson & Ann Mary Holland
	July 19	Thos. Abrams & Betsy Simmons

1817	Aug. 23	Thos. Coe & Ann Durye
	Sep. 4	Robt. Wilson & Matilda Couwenhoven
	Oct. 5	-----? Farrington & ------? Mills
	Oct. 9	Wm. Bennet & Cath. Wykof
	Oct. 15	Lucas Emans & Patty Eldert
	Dec. 6	Chas. Debevoise & Ann Debevoise
	Dec. 10	Thos. Stoothoff & Peggy Mills
1818	Jan. 11	St. Laun & Eliz. Hudson
	Jan. 24	Saml. Demott & Polly Coevert
	April 2	Cors. V. Brunt & Aletta Smith
	May 30	Simon Cornell & Maria Cortelyou
	July 5	John V. Derbourgh & Hannah Baiseley
	July 21	Chas. Hepburn & Maria Chardavoyne; both of New York
	Sep. 17	Nich. R. Cornell & Ann Adelia Wells
	Dec. 11	Wm. Rhodes & Polly Wright

1818	Dec. 11	Hoyt Creed & Cath. Lane
	Dec. 29	Saml. Williams & Jane Durye
1819	Feb. 14	Capt. Peter Couwenhoven & Mrs. Cath. V. Dyke (She of Red Hook)
	Feb. 20	Benj. Moore & Sally Creed
	March 8	Nich. Lott & Adriana Snedeker
	May 20	John Oakley & Charity Hendickson
	May 25	Wm. Craig & Mary Pritchard
	Aug. 21	John Smith & Eliz. Cornish
	Aug. 5	Garret Nostrand & Sally Bennet
	Sep. 2	Hewlett Creed & Ann Hicks
	Sep. 5	Wm. H. Cornell & Eliz. Doughty
	Sep. 30	Wm. Hendickson & Phebe Golder
	Oct. 16	John Ryerson & Susanna V. Nostrand
	Nov. 11	Rich. Rhodes & Fanny Smith

1819	Nov. 11	Rich V. Brunt & Maria Tuthill
	Dec. 18	Aug. Durscher & Maria Patten
1820	Jan. 15	Chas. West & Eleanor Slavin
	Feb. 3	Jacob Storm & Cath. Rapelye; daughter of Jacob of N. T.
	Feb. 19	Jona. Morrel & Rebecca Wortman
	March 5	Isaac Eldert & Sarah Ann Cozyne
	Mar. 11	Arthur Guthrie & Sarah Gray
	Mar. 20	Uriah Hendikson & Ida Lott
	April 10	Saml. V. Buren & Sally Debevoise
	April 15	Jas. Vassar & Eliz. Bond
	April 22	Dominicus Snedeker & Phebe Suydam
	May 10	Abm. Bergen & Winifred Hendrikson
	May 20	Jas. Areson & Matilda Areson
	July 16	Saml. Messenger & Margaret Roe

1820	Aug. 12	Chas. Thompson & Mary Denton
	Aug. 23	John Golder & Patty Golder
	Aug. 26	Isaac Bond & Ellen V. Derburgh
	Sep. 10	Henry Stoothof & Eliza. Titus
	Dec. 17	Jos. Tompkins & Betsy Springsteen
	Dec. 30	John Vail & Ellen Billings
1821	Jan. 4	Martin Rapelye & Eliz. Larremore
	Jan. 25	John Remsen & Altie Hendikson
	April 5	Jas. Rapelye & Ann Remsen
	April 9	Wm. Paynter & Mary Ann V. Alst ?
	April 21	Simeon Fosdick & Aletta Remsen
	June 2	Nehemiah C. Nafis & Maria Cornish
	June 6	Danl. Lent & Jane Remsen
	July 12	Capt. Jas. Schoonmaker & Mary Ann Skidmore

1821	July 16	Furman Romans & Ann Underhill
	July 26	John Sutphin & Peggy Wykof
	Sep. 11	Thos. Lott & Jane V. Pelt
	Sep. 29	Simon Gildersleve & Ruth Gessner
	Oct. 13	Thos. Lane & Cath. Snedeker
	Nov. 1	Jacobus Kolyer & Eliz. Wortman
	Dec. 1	Jeremiah Scouton & Mrs. Loretta Areson
	Dec. 17	John V. deveer Simonson & Ann Blake
	Dec. 22	Jacob M. Durye & Ida Sprong
	Dec. 31	David D. Bayard & Eliza Boerum
1822	Jan. 5	Daniel Powel & Matilda Anderson
	Jan. 9	Jas. Nesbit & Sarah Monfort
	Jan. 14	Geo. J. Rapelye & Margaret Colyer
	Jan. 27	Jacob Ryerson & Lydia Folk

1822	Mar. 7	Jas. Baylis & Betsy Hendickson
	Mar. 14	Jacob Snedeker & Ann Lott
	April 11	Benj. Hegeman & Sarah Durye
	May 15	And. Gorsline & Gertrude Leverick
	June 13	Hewlett Townsend Coles & Cath. Suydam
	June 26	Isaac Hincksman & Hester Pettit
	Aug. 25	And. Pettit & Eliz. Fabel
	Oct. 1	Cors. E. Scoffie & Eliza Bloom
	Oct. 27	Geo. V. Brunt & Jane ? Cornell
	"	Peter Durye & Jane ? Cornell
	Nov. 17	Nathl. Rhodes & Maria Searles
	Dec. 18	Bernardus Bloom & Mrs. Eliza Hatfield
	Dec. 19	Owen Mallen & Nauchie Beckwith
1823	Jan. 22	John Oakley & Ann Debevoise

1823	Feb. 2	Walter Way & Helena V. Wicklen
	Feb. 17	Jas. Turner & Hannah Rider
	Mar. 19	Alex. Davison & Amelia Denton
	April 3	John B. Martin & Sally A. Henderson
	April 9	Williamson Rapelye & Ann Vanderveer
	April 24	Geo. Rhodes & Eliza Hicks
	May 11	Saml. Burtis & Eliza Coe
	May 30	Saml. Simmons & -----? Allen
	June 4	S----? Thornton & Jemima Bond
	Sep. 17	Underhill Covert & Jane Schenk
	Oct. 19	Robt. Coe & Fanny Phillips
	Nov. 1	Geo. Hoogland & Ann V. Sicklen
	Nov. 15	Abm. V. Sicklen & Phebe Wykof
	Nov. 16	Benj. Sammis & Maria Lott

1823	Dec. 17	Saml. Cornell & Betsy Pearsall
	Dec. 18	St. Lott & Cornelis Snedeker
	Dec. 29	Rem Lefferts Maria Brower
1824	Jan. 8	John Nesbit & Phebe Bennet
	Jan. 23	Wm. Hendrikson & Maria Bennet
	Feb. 12	Smith Everit Hend'kson & Susan Rider
	April 8	Dow D. Rapelye & Cataline Suydam
	April 24	Wm. Lewis & Jane Simmons
	---------	Remsen Simmons & Betsy Frederick
	Aug. 18	Abner Chichester & Agnes Conklin
	Sep. 9	Ralph Howard & Eliza Cozyne
	Sep. 12	John Schureman & Margaret Remsen
	Oct. 8	Saml. Shindler & Eliza Weeden
	Oct. 15	Lawrence Watts & Eliz. Hendickson

1824	Oct. 21	Hudson V. Sinderen & Ione Ann Durye
	Oct. 26	David Frederick & Jane Lambertson
	Nov. 3	Danl. Remsen & Hannah Hicks
	Nov. 28	John Hunter, Jr. & Cath. Devosteny
	Dec. 1	John Cozyne & Eliz. Rumph
	Dec. 16	Geo. Watts & Phebe Golder
	Dec. 30	Saml. Way & Maria Miller
1825	Feb. 6	Isaac V. deveer & Eliz. V. Pelt
	March 16	Gerrit Stoothof & Aletta Smith
	April 6	Burling Folk & Cath. Ann Colyer
	April 20	Nathl. Mills & Altie Hendrikson
	April 27	John Titus & Maria Hardenbergh
	June 28	Jas. Higbie & Ann Stoothof
	July 6	Obadiah Valentine & Phebe Higbie

1825	Sep. 7	St. Decker & Hannah V. Arsdalen
	Nov. 2	Saml. Valentine & Maria Riker
	Nov. 9	Nathl. Mills & Sarah Ann Everitt
	Nov. 12	Geo. W. Dodge & Mary Brown
	Dec. 15	Woodhull Hicks & Ida Everitt
	Dec. 21	Jas. Debevoise & Hetty Bragan
	Dec. 22	Derick Amerman & Eliz. Stoothof
	Dec. 22	Wm. Ludlum & Cath. Rhodes
	Dec. 25	Chas. Turnbull & Mary Snedeker
1826	Jan. 28	Albert Silliman & Eliza Rhodes
	Jan. 29	Isaac Bird & Sarah Springsteen
	---- ?	John N. Mills & Jane Durye
	March 2	Aury Amerman & Hannah Amerman
	April 19	John Colyer & Rachel Way

1826	April 29	Wm. Fowler & Aletta Holmes
	May 18	Ezra Palmer & Phebe Bennet
	July 6	Garret V. Dine & Hannah Demot
	July 16	Jas. V. deveer & Aletta Diddle
	July 26	Amy R. Golder & Mary Mills
	Aug. 2	Jacob Boerum & Aletta Durye
	Aug. 5	Obadiah Booth & Maria Manning
	Aug. 29	Thos. Benson & Sarah Jones
	Sep. 4	Robt. W. Stoddart & Mary Ann Areson
	Sep. 7	Wm. Golder & Phebe Golder
	Sep. 20	Danl. Cornell & Eva Cath. Rapelye
	Sep. 30	Seth Bruce & Mary Tower
	Oct. 8	Chas. Lafetra & Martha Eliz. V. Lew
	Oct. 25	Wm. Stoothof & Lydia Ryerson

1826	Oct. 26	Saml. Nichol & Louisa Plane
	Dec. 6	Geo. Rapelye & Jane Maria Suydam
	Dec. 14	Benj. F. Willets & Sally Rapelye
	Dec. 20	John Rhodes & Aletta Bennet
1827	Jan. 28	Smith Dorland & Ann Williamson
	Jan. 31	Rich. Way, Jr. & Patty Maria Pell
	Feb. 5	Jas. Denise & Rachel V. de graw
	Feb. 6	Skidmore V. Nostrand & Sally Ann Hendickson
	Feb. 14	Jesse Mills & Ann Golder
	Feb. 14	Foster Hendickson & Ann Remsen
	April 12	Obadiah Schenck & Elizabeth Griffin
	April 18	Johnson Selover & Margaret Ryder
	April 19	Thos. Allen & Mrs. Ann Stoothoff
	May 22	Henry Murray & Jane Dorland

1827	June 17	Lewis Conklin & Eliza Carpenter
	June 27	Henry Eldert & Sarah Coles
	Aug. 5	Elijah Hendrkson & Maria Snedeker
	Aug. 7	Cors. Peterson & Sarah Ann Simonson
	Aug. 11	Nicholas Cashow & Phebe Field
	Sep. 19	Matthew T. Van Zandt & Maria Suydam
	Sep. 25	Jas. Reeves & Mary Baylis
	Nov. 6	Peter Nostrand & Margaret Lott
	Dec. 11	Robt. T. Lawrence & Phebe Jane Mead
	Dec. 12	Isaac Bragan & Cornelia Duryea
	Dec. 31	Lott Wykoff & Sarah Lott
1828	Jan. 28	Wm. Williamson & Cath. Ryder
	Feb. 12	Johannis Colyer & Eliz. Remsen
	Feb. 13	Benj. Hoogland & Eliza V. Alst

1828	Feb. 24	John Wiggins & Jane Remsen
	March 5	John Messenger & Johana Hendikson
	April 3	Jos. Way & Cornelia Covert
	April 26	Tim. Rhodes & Peggy Bennet
	May 9	John L. Boyd & Gertrude Rapelye
	May 31	Richard Case & Cath. Ann Pettit
	June 22	Tunis Dorlant & Ruth Cornell
	Aug. 4	Alex. Robertson & Mary Ann Lawrence
	Aug. 9	Isaac Sorals & Jane Durye
	Sep. 19	Chas. Poling & Mary Ann V. Sicklen
	Sep. 20	Hend'k Sonals & Hannah Ann Cozine
	Oct. 11	John Remson & Betsy Hendricks
	Nov. 16	Danl. Colyer & Maria Morrel
	Dec. 23	Scott Bowne & Emely Ann Hendrikson

1828	Dec. 24	Chas. Hallock & Aletta Remsen
1829	Jan. 14	Danl. Hendrikson & Hannah Cortelyou
	Jan. 21	Increase Carpenter & Charity Ann Hendickson
	Jan. 30	John Golder & Harriet Cornell
	Feb. 11	St. Mills & Sally Hendrikson
	Mar. 11	Isaac Bowne & Deborah Durye
	Mar. 11	Danl. Brinkerhof & Phebe Bogart
	Mar. 29	Jona. Bennett & Eliz. Snedeker
	Mar. 30	Geo. B. Brinkerhof & Sarah Ann Colyer
	May 20	Wm. Golder & Sarah Golder
	-------	Hanford Mead & Harriet Ann Eldert
	April 27	Jas. Reeve & Mary Creed
	Aug. 3	Wm. M. Smith & Nelly Bennet
	Aug. 6	John Thatford & Cornelia Bennet

1829	Sep. 4	Jas. B. Griffin & Susan T. Forman
	Sep. 30	Geo. Nostrand & Eliz. Nostrand
	Oct. 24	Thos. Pettit & Johanna Smith
	Nov. 1	Wm. W. Hankison & Eliza V. Horn
	Nov. 7	Abm. Barker & Eliza V. Siclen
	Nov. 10	John Brush & Peggy Golder
1830	Jan. 26	Henry Mills, Jamaica: aged 19 & Cath. Ann Hendickson of Jamaica, aged 18
	Jan. 27	Chas. Berry of Jamaica; aged 26 & Jane Golder of Jamaica; aged 17
	Mar. 18	Ludlum Frederick of Jamaica, Carpenter; aged 24 & Eliz. Smith of Jamaica; aged 20
	Mar. 18	Wm. Mott of Hempstead; aged 21 & Ann Hewlett of Hempstead; aged 18
	April 8	Cors. Ackerman of New York, Merchant; aged 18 & Eliz. Ennis of New York, aged 17
	April 18	St. Ryder of Jamaica; aged 21 & Ann Ryder of Jamaica, aged 18

1830 April 23   Robt. McCormick of Flushing, Carpenter; aged 37 & Mary Young of Flushing, aged 25

May 12   Elias Hendrikson of N. U., aged 27 & Charity Simonson of Jamaica; aged 18 yrs

May 29   John Berger of N. Br., Merchant & Phebe Totten of New Town

Aug. ---   Mathias Ackerman of New York, Cart., aged 47 & Jane Wood of Hempstead, aged 43

Sep. 19   Albert Amerman of Jamaica; aged 40 & Maria Marsten of Jamaica, aged 30

Oct. 14   Willet Wickes of Brooklyn, Shoemaker, aged 24 & Matilda Carpenter of Brooklyn, aged 24

Nov. 29   John Suydam of Flushing, aged 27 & Eliz. Snedeker of Jamaica, mantua maker; aged 24

Dec. 6   Jas. Denton of Jamaica, butcher, aged 21 and Jane Durye of Jamaica, aged 18

Dec. 22   Elwin Hyatt of New Town; aged 27 & Julia Gorsline of New Town; aged 25

1831	Jan. 5	Benj. Wiggins of No. Hempstead, aged 24 and Amelia Ann Bergen, So. Hempstead; aged 15 ½ years
	Jan. 12	Remsen Smith of Jamaica, aged 23 & Cath. Hendikson of Jamaica, aged 21
	Jan. 25	Danl. Smith of Jamaica; aged 23 & Ann Frederick of Jamaica, aged 15
	Feb. 23	Thos. Smith, aged 26 & Mary Amberman of Jamaica, aged 18 years
	Mar. 28	Seth R. Fox of New York, Coppersmith, aged 22 & Martha Lines of New York, aged 23
	June 2	Saml. R. B. Norton of So. Hempstead, aged 22 & Ann Gibson of New York; aged 18
	June 21	Danl. Smith of Jamaica, aged 21 and Priscilla Hendrickson, aged 22
	July 2	Oldfield Bergen & Abigail Cornell of So. Hempstead
	July 6	Saml. Dunn of Brooklyn, aged 24 & Eliza Sinclair of Brooklyn, aged 18
	July 13	Walter Griffin of Flushing; aged 23 & Ellen Griffin of Flushing, aged 32

1831	Oct. 15	Abm. Emmons, Gr. f., & Sarah V. Pelt
	Nov. 5	Edward Field of Flushing, aged 26 & Ann Reyer of Flushing; aged 28
	Dec. 6	Albert Snedeker of Jamaica, aged 27 & Polly Smith of Jamaica, aged 27
	Dec. 21	Abm. Giffin of Jamaica & Aletta Jane Dorland of Jamaica
	Dec. 21	Abm. Snedeker of New Lots & Cecilia Wright of New Lots
	Dec. 24	Geo. Pine of N. T. & Agnes Durye of N. T.
1832	Feb. 8	W. G. Carpenter & Cornelia Bennet)
		) Twins
	"	W. I. Carpenter & Phebe Bennet)
	Mar. 14	Abm. Bergen of Flushing & Sally Brown of Flushing
	Mar. 27	Wm. Hendrickson of Jamaica & Dorothy Remsen of Jamaica
	May 20	Philip French of New York; aged 22 & Joanna Sannon of New York, aged 20
	July 3	Jas. Raynor, Innkeeper, Brooklyn & Eliza Shay of New York

1832	Aug. 1	Jos. Fish of Groton aged 23 & Cath Brush of Jamaica, aged 21
	Aug. 6	Warren Mundy of N. T. & Abby Simmons of N. T.
	Aug. 28	C. Hendrikson of Jamaica & Ann Remsen of Jamaica
	Oct. 25	Cors. Bennet of Jamaica & Maria Hendikson of F. M.
	Oct. 31	Hiram Kipp of New York & Miss Theoland Hartwell of New York; daughter of Stephen H.
	Nov. 19	Aury Bennet of Jamaica & Eliz. Hicks of Flushing
	Dec. 6	Abm. Fleet of Jamaica & Martha Eliza Lafetre of Jamaica
1833	Jan. 1	Remsen Bennet of Jamaica & Mary Ann Smith of Jamaica
	Jan. 16	Isaac Bennet of Jamaica & Sarah Pettit of Jamaica
	Jan. 17	Cors. Bennet of Flushing & Eliz. Smith of Flushing
	Jan. 28	Isaac Brush of F. M. & Martha Langdon of F. M.

1833   Feb. 20   Wm. V. Siclen of Hempstead & Sarah Eliz. Hendickson of Jamaica

Feb. 27   John Smith of Flushing & Jane Eliza V. Wicklen of N. T.

Feb. 8   Abm. Sypher of Flushing & Abigail Lum of Brooklyn

Mar. 19   John Schenk of Brooklyn, Merchant & Eliza Remsen of N. T.

April 23   Nich. Wykof of Jamaica & Betsy V. Brunt, widow of Garret Bennet

May 1   Saml. Frederiks of Jamaica & Hannah Francis of Jamaica
        Brothers
"   John Frederiks of Jamaica & Jane Coles of Jamaica

May 29   Saml. Powell of Hempstead & Ellen Marrten of Jamaica

June 26   Ferdinand Snediker of Jamaica & Eliza Suydam of Flushing

Aug. 18   Moses V. Baldwin of Brooklyn & Lucy Carman of Rockaway

Sep. 2   John Colyer of Bushwick & Phebe Ann Hoyt of N. T.

1833	Sep. 21	Skidmore Selover of Jamaica & Maria Demott of F. M.
	Oct. 18	Johnson Eldert of Brooklyn & Phebe Ryerson of New Lots
	Oct. 14	Manuel T. Texido of Flushing & Mary C. Bird of Flushing
	Oct. 19	Lorenzo North of N. T. & Priscilla Atwater of Troy
	Oct. 23	David Allen of Jamaica & Mary Snedeker of Jamaica
	Oct. 29	And. Reid of Rich., Virginia & Eliz. Curr of Jamaica
	Nov. –	John V. Siclen of Hempstead & Eliz. Jane Remsen
	Nov. 6	Jacob Howe of Jamaica & Aletta Jane V. Lew of Jamaica
	Nov. 18	Silvester Moore of Newark & Hetty Malvina Peshire of Newark, N. J.
	Dec. 4	John Powell of No. Hempstead & Peggy Marston of Jamaica

1833	Dec. 11	Jas. Nostrand of Jamaica & Eliz Allen of Jamaica
	Dec. 12	Jas. Stoddard of Brooklyn & Cath. Nostrand of Brooklyn
	Dec. 18	Benj. C. Byrd of Flushing & Eliz. B. Bowne of Flushing
	Dec. 23	Jas. Lawrence of Flushing & Phebe Skidmore of Flushing
1834	Jan. 1	Rich. Hunter of N. T. & Jane V. Alst of Dutch Kills
	Jan. 8	John H. Hendickson of Jamaica & Susan Allen of Jamaica
	Jan. 22	Anselm H. Conklin of Jamaica & Ellen Suydam of N. T.
	Feb. 1	Jos. Pearsall of Rockaway & Mary Eliz. Abrams of Rockaway
	Feb. 26	John G. V. Alst of N. T. & Nelly Debevoise of N. T.
	Mar. 5	Geo. Rowland of Jamaica & Aletta Smith of Jamaica

1834	May 1	Saml. Titus of New York & Addria Ann Cortelyou of Flushing
	May 14	Barzillai Hammond of N. T. & Mary Poling of Jamaica
	Aug. 24	Edward F. Furman of N. T. & Jane Denton of N. T.
	Aug. 31	Rich. Whipple of Brooklyn & Mary Jane Morris of N. T.
	Sep. 3	John Bergen of Jamaica & Phebe R. Snedeker of Jamaica
	Sep. 8	Chas. H. Woods of Philadelphia & Margaret Brinkerhof of Jamaica
1835	Mar. 22	Thos. Everdell of N. T. & Cath. Hipwell (widow Lowe) of N. T.
	Mar. 23	Cors. M. Rapelye of G. N. & Cath. H. Allen of Great Neck
	April 22	Hendk. Hendrikson of Jamaica & Annetie Brinkerhof of Brooklyn
	Dec. 16	Oldfield Hendikson of Jamaica & Margaret V. Alst of N. T.

1836	April 6	David West of Flushing & Mary Ann Fish of Flushing
1837	Jan. 5	Martin Suydam of N. T. & Helena Henrietta Schoonmaker of Jamaica
1835	Nov. 25	Benj. Wright of Flushing & Eliza Ann Miller of Flushing
	July 5	Chas. Ball of Waterford & Eliza Card of Waterford
	July 30	Wm. Amerman of Jamaica & Jane V. Zant of Albany
	Sep. 23	Jeremiah V. Brunt of Jamaica & Cath. Durye of Jamaica
	Nov. 5	John Willet of Flushing & Margaret Willet of Flushing
	Dec. 1	Gerardres Martin of Jamaica & Margaret Jackson of Jamaica
1836	Jan. 13	Wm. Alfred Valentine of Flushing & Frances Emily Carll of Jamaica
	Feb. 7	John M. Myers of Brooklyn & Susan Doxey of Jamaica

1836	Mar. 16	Wm. Dorland of Brooklyn & Mary Ann Golder of Jamaica
	April 27	Jos. Willet of Flushing & Almira West of Flushing
	June 4	Wm. I. Golder of Jamaica & Eliz. Nostrand of New York
	Aug. 15	John N. Sharpe of New York & Ann Sharp of New York
	Sep. 22	Thos. Foster of Jamaica & Margaret Frederiks of Jamaica
	Sep. 28	Isaac Hendickson of Flushing & Charity Durye of Flushing
	Oct. 2	David Harris of Jamaica & Jane Wiggins, widow of Cors. Eldert, of Jamaica
	Nov. 16	Geo. D. Pershire of Newark & Margaret Merlette of Newark
	Dec. 7	Geo. Carpenter of New York & Sarah Ann Bennet of Jamaica
	Dec. 18	Wm. Smith Mayhew of Jamaica & Margaret Julia V. Lew of Jamaica

1836	Dec. 25	Heroin W. Woodruff of Harlem & Sarah Ann Howe of Harlem
1837	Jan. 4	Nathl. Nostrand of Jamaica & Phebe Hendikson of Jamaica
	Jan. 5	John V. Wicklen of Jamaica & Phebe Ann Youngs
	Jan. 22	Danl. Allen of Jamaica & Eliza Martin of Jamaica
	Sep. 13	John N. Briggs of New York & Gertrude Suydam
1838	Feb. 8	Richard Smith of Far Rockaway & mary Ann Wanser of ?
	Mar. 14	Peter Hendrikson of New Town & Eliz. C. Schoonmaker of Jamaica
	Mar. 19	Wm. Sefton of New York & Ann Waring of New York
	Mar. 28	Jas. Howell Lodge of Jamaica & Eliz. Smith of Jamaica
	April 19	Geo. F. Carmen of Jamaica & Harriet Bennet of Jamaica

1838	May 19	Abm. Folk of New Town & Eliza Burdett
	June 18	Kirkbride Drake of New York & Aletta Sweet of Jamaica
	July 23	Abm Ayres of Jamaica & Madeline V. Lew
	Sep 3	Abm Mills of New York & Maria Rapelye of Jamaica
	Sep. 13	John R. Briggs of New York & Getty Suydam of New Town
	Oct. 24	Jas. Higbie of Jamaica & Mary Covert of Jamaica
	Nov. 11	Garret V. Wicklen of New Town & Cath. Smith
	Nov. 16	Jas. Hendickson of Hempstead & Ann Smith of Fos. M.
1838	Feb. 29	Rev. R. L. Schoonmaker of Jamaica & Margaret Seaman of Jamaica
	Mar. 24	Jas. A. Cummings of Jamaica & Eliza Mullen of Jamaica
	Mar. 25	Henry C. Ham & Anna Maria Gorman of Jamaica
	Mar. 31	Walter Peck of New Lots & Sarah Simonson, widow of John V. Wicklen

1838	April 5	Saml. A. Purdy, M.D., of New York & Ann Maria Palmer of Jamaica
	April 22	Chas. W. Merrit of New York & Ann V. Vleck
	June 24	Isaac Morrel of Jamaica & Rebecca Bliss of New York
	June 28	Robt. Wanser of Flushing & Cath. Field of Flushing
	July 4	John Watts & Phebe Simonson
	Oct. 4	Isaac Greene of Williamsburgh & Eliz. Pashley
	Oct. 12	Jeremiah Watts & Abigail Ryder
	Nov. 1	John C. Brink of New York & Rebecca Ann Marshall of New Town
1837	Dec. 13	Thos. J. Cornell & Ann V. Nostrand, both of Success
	"	Jno. Stoothof of Jamaica & Elsie Williamson of Jamaica S.
	Dec. 27	Benj. J. Smith of Bushwick & widow Ann Maria Hendrikson

1838	Jan. 10	Jeromus V. Nuys of Flatlands & Ann Eliza Brinkerhof of Jamaica
	Dec. 4	Hendrikson Creed of Jamaica & Jane D. Remsen Wiggins, widow of John Wiggins of Jamaica
	Dec. 19	Wm. Wright of Flushing & Mary J. Cornwell of Flushing
	Dec. 25	Danl. Macon of N. T. & Mary Agnes V. Dine of N. T.
1839	Jan. 2	Nathl. Tilton of N. T. & Amelia Ann Remsen of N. T.
	Jan. 30	Jos. Demonte of Jamaica & Sarah Eliz. Bergen of Jamaica
	Feb. 27	Oliver Lawrence of No. Hempstead & Margaret Ann Rogers
	March 12	Rev. G. I. Garretson of N. T. & Cath. Rapelye of N. T.
	May 1	Wm. Stoothof of New Lots & Sarah Stoothof of Jamaica
	May 15	Saml. Skidmore of Flushing & Mary Eliza Tyson of Jamaica
	"	Wm. Phraner & Ellen Marie V. derveer

1839	May 22	Saml. Eldert & Aletta Ann Stoothof
	May 24	Strong Conklin of Plains' & Sarah Hicks of Plains. John Tredwell, witness
	June 3	Chas. Coles of Boston & Ann Bradlee of Jamaica
	July 12	Gustavus A. Crane of Flushing & Abigail Areson, widow of Wm. Pinkham of Flushing
	Aug. 5	John Welling of Jamaica & Hannah Tuthill of Jamaica
	"	Saml. Wells Bowker of Rockaway & Aletta Ann Morgan of Rockaway
	Sep. 5	Horatio Nelson Fitzgerald of New York & Susan Bruce of Jamaica
	Sep. 10	Nich. Emmons of Jamaica & Cath. Baiseley of Jamaica
	Oct. 9	John L. Denton of Flushing & Ann Spader of Jamaica
	Oct. 22	Squire A. Smith of Flushing & Lucy Lawson of New York

1839	Nov. 14	Jacob R. Schenk of Great Neck Martha S. Burtis of Manhasset
	Nov. 18	Chas. J. Hubbs of Harlem & Eliz. Adelia V. Cott of Jamaica
	Dec. 11	John B. Lott of Jamaica & Mary Denton of Flushing
	Dec. 12	Wm. R. Siney of New York & Ida Ann Bergen of Flushing
	Dec. 17	Abm. Mills of New York & Ellen Lott of Jamaica
	Dec. 30	Martin J. Johnson of Jamaica & Eliza Ditmars of Jamaica
1840	Jan. 21	Alfred H. Munroe of Rhode Island & Rachel Remsen of Jamaica
	Jan. 22	Nich. Ludlum of F. M. & Sarah Eliz. V. Nostrand of F. M.
	Feb. 4	Chas. Abrams Frederick of Jamaica & Sarah Jane Smith of Jamaica
	Feb. 5	Danl. Rapelye of N. T. & Hannah V. Dine of Hempstead Plains

1840	Mar. 25	John Everit of Jamaica & Eliza Welling of Jamaica
	June 25	St. Murphy of F. M. & Eliza N. Higbie of Spr'd
	July 4	Rich. Amberman of Sp. & Cornelia Cornell of Plains
	Aug. 2	Thos. Cornwell of Jamaica & Martha Ann Rhodes of Jamaica
	Sep. 17	Wm. H. Woolley of Jamaica & Joanna K. Van Sicklen of Jamaica
	Oct. 11	Alex Parkes of Flushing & Ellen Slater of Flushing
	Oct. 22	Rich. Deremer of Jamaica & Sarah Eldert of Jamaica
	Nov. 10	Robert Allen of Jamaica & Aletta I. Snedeker of Jamaica
	Nov. 11	Jas. Lott of Jamaica & Hester Osterman of Flushing
	Nov. 25	Wm. Hegeman of Bushwick & Emma Remsen of N. T.
1841	Jan. 10	Jona. W. Smith of Jamaica & Eliz. Areson of Jamaica

1841	Feb. 17	John Allen of Jamaica & Sarah Monfort of Jamaica
	May 12	Dr. Wm. D. Creed of Jamaica & Maria Mills, widow of S. Hendrikson
	May 26	Ezra Miller of Flushing & Amanda J. Miller of Westchester County
	June 8	Alonzo Carll of Flushing & Mary Ann Buffit of Flushing
	Sep. 18	Hendrik Dorland of Jamaica & Nelly Jane Williamson of Jamaica
	Oct. 19	Saml. C. Hendickson of O. B. & Eliz. Valentine of Flushing
	Nov. 3	Jos. Macoon of N. T. & Sarah Jane Morrell of N. T.
	Nov. 21	John Foster of No. Hempstead & Cath. C. Cornell of No. Hempstead
	Dec. 22	John Starkins of Flushing & Sarah Zellor of Jamaica
1842	Feb. 9	Jno. R. Simonson of Brooklyn & Margaret Ann V. Dine of Jamaica
	Feb. 17	Hugh Conklin of Jamaica & Sarah Youngs of Jamaica

1842	Mar. 8	Anthony Wright of Hempstead & Charity Ann Amberman of Jamaica
	Mar. 30	John J. Watts of Rockaway & Susan Tyler of Rockaway
	---------	Wm. B. Fowler of Flushing & Sarah Bass of Flushing
	April 27	Jas. L. Smith of Jamaica & Hannah Remsen of Jamaica
	June 7	Jacob Lawrence of Rockaway & Nelly Smith of Rockaway
	Sep. 3	Chas. Abrams of Rockaway & Cath. Naid of Rockaway
	Oct. 13	Abm. Hendrikson of Flushing & Hannah Simonson of Spr.
	Nov. 8	John Smith of Spr. & Sarah Ann Nostrand of Spr.
	Nov. 30	Wm. Fosdick of Spr. & Hannah Henderson of Jamaica South
	Dec. 6	Wm. Parsons of Jamaica & Cath. Burke of Jamaica
	Dec. 7	Jas. Aug. Herriman of Jamaica & Jane Seaman of Jamaica

1842	Dec. 27	John Doremus of Flushing & Ellen Snedeker of Jamaica
	Dec. 28	Geo. Valentine of Flushing & Anna Barbara Doremus of Flushing
1843	Feb. 22	Martin Courten of Flushing & Fanny Ann Speelden of Flushing
	Mar. 1	Geo. Bennet of Spr. & Jane Eliz. Carpenter of Jamaica
	Nov. 12	Wm. French of Flushing & Sarah Moore of Jamaica
	July 4	Wm. Raynor of H? & Jane Sorrel of H--?
	Sep. 10	Benj. H. Cornell of Flushing & Mary Eliz. Fowler of Flushing
	Sep. 19	Jas. W. Valentine of Rockaway H. & Sarah Prevoost of Bushwick
	Oct. 22	Wm. T. V. Nostrand of Brooklyn & Mehitable Bradlee of Jamaica
	Nov. 8	Henry Drew of New Lots & Sarah Lott of Jamaica
	Nov. 22	Burdett Douglas of Jamaica & Charity H. Remsen of Jamaica

1843	Dec. 27	Jos. Powell of Jamaica & Jane Lott of Jamaica
1844	Feb. 14	John D. Snedeker of Jamaica & Jane Amanda Nelson of Jamaica
	Feb. 25	Saml. Way of N. T. & Maria Snedeker, widow of -------- Hendrikson
	Mar. 1	Adam Moser of Jamaica & Eliza Ann Nelson of Jamaica
	Mar. 10	Robt. P. Field of Jamaica & Eliza Vassar of Jamaica
	Mar. 13	Saml. Stryket Lott of Flatlands & Hannah Ann Ryder of Jamaica
	April 14	Carr Hubbs of Jamaica & Harriet Louisa V. Lew of Jamaica
	May 1	Jesse D. Wright of Jamaica & Louisa Henderson of Jamaica
	May 28	Jas. A. Roe of Flushing & Rebecca Tomkins of N. T.
	Mar. 20	Benj. Curtis & Eliz. Nostrand (col'd. ?)
	Aug. 28	Bernardus Bennet of Jamaica & Eliz. Mary Hendrickson of Spr'd.

1844	Sep. 4	Rich. Hendickson of Hempstead & Phebe S. Remsen of Jamaica
	Sep. 24	St. Henderson of Jamaica & Eliz. Martin of Jamaica
	Oct. 15	Jos. Mills of Jamaica & Ann Bergen Remsen
	Oct. 23	Evert V. Wicklen of Jamaica & Margaret Eldert of Jamaica
	Nov. 20	John H. Cornell of Flushing & Matilda Loweree of Flushing
	Nov. 27	Jas. Duncan of Flushing & Eliz. V. Wicklen, widow of John Abrams of Flushing
	Nov. 28	Ephraim R. Shaw of Hudson & Sarah B. Story of Jamaica
	Dec. 12	Michael Springsteen of N. T. & Aletta Durye of Jamaica
1845	Jan. 18	Henry Nostrand of Hempstead & Eliza V. Lew of Hempstead
	Jan. 22	Isaac Morrel of N. T. & Eliz. McCoun of N. T.
	Mar. 30	Thos. Hyatt of N. T. & Mary Eliz. Forble of New Lots

1845	May 21	Benj. Hegeman of Flushing & Maria Duryea of Flushing
	July 19?	Jeremiah Cheshire of Jamaica & Margaret Ann Bergen of Jamaica
	June 11	Sam. H. Demott of Jamaica & Cath. Jane Smith of Jamaica
	Sep. 4	Rich. Thorn of Flushing & Mary Simonson of Jamaica
	Nov. 5	Jos. Oldfield Bergen of F. M. & Sarah R. Rhodes of Flushing
	Nov. 13	Wm. Henry Ryerson of Flushing & Cornelia Fish of Flushing
	Dec. 10	Henry Suydam of New York & Ellen S. Hegeman of Flushing
	Dec. 16	Jas. Everitt of Jamaica & Sarah Rogers of Jamaica
	"	Henry Lott of Jamaica & Cataline Eldert of Jamaica
1846	Jan. 5	Wm. B. Waters of New Lots & Ellen Cozyn of New Lots
	Jan. 8	Jas. Hendickson of Spr. & Cath. Hendickson of Spr.

1846	Mar. 24	Edward D. Leary of Brooklyn & Hannah Woodruff of Brooklyn
	April 14	Cors. Rhodes of Flushing & ?? Hallet
	May 21	Geo. W. Thorne of Jamaica & Sarah Ann Creed of Jamaica
	June 23	Chas. Poulson of New York & Lydia V. Wicklen of Jamaica
	June 28	Benj. Denton of Jamaica South & Mary Ann Hitchcock of Jamaica South
	Nov. 20	John Livingston of New Lots & Maria L. Wykof of New Town
	Oct. 6	Wm. E. Valentine of Flushing & Phebe E. Kissam of Flushing
	Oct. 20	Wm. Kouwenhoven of N. T. & Phebe Maria Durye of Jamaica
	Dec. 30	Wyckof Drew of N. Lots & Sarah Ann Deneboise of N. T.
1847	Feb. 6	Israel Youngs of Flushing & Alicia Boughton of Flushing
	Feb. 16	Albert Stoothof of Jamaica & Sarah Murray

1847	Feb. 9	Saml. Bouton of Jamaica & Getty Snedeker of Jamaica
	April 12	Philip Wagner of Jamaica & Catherine Emily -------?
	Nov. 9	John Godkin of Jamaica & Susan Smith of Spr.
	July 4	Rich. Bishop & Cath. Mott
	Dec. 23	John R. Siney of New York & Cath. L. Wykoff of N. T.
	July 4	John H. Schoonmaker of Jamaica, aged 22 and Sarah Willis of Jamaica aged 21
	-------	Jona. D. Hull of N. Lebanon, aged 21 & Anna B. Schoonmaker of Jamaica, aged 21
1848	Jan. 7	Wm. Foster of Flushing & Ida A. Sprong of Flushing
	Feb. 22	Geo. Page of New York & Rebeca McCoun of N. T.
	April 9	Mat. M. Totten of Jamaica & Cath. A. Leach
	May 9	Cors. V. Dine of New York & Jane R. Schoonmaker of Jamaica

1848	May 25	Jeremiah Johnson of Brooklyn & Maria Johnson of Jamaica
	July 4	Lott Simonson of ? & Eliz. Amerman of Jamaica
	July 4	Jas. H. Fleury of N. T. & Hannah Maria Seaman of Jamaica
	Aug. 20	Geo. Miller of Jamaica & Sarah Eliza Brinkerhof of Jamaica
	"	Jacob Grater of Jamaica & Jane Ann Brinkerhof of Jamaica
	Sep. 3	John B. Lott of Spr. & Ellen Jessup of Jamaica
	Dec. 13	Thos. B. Lamberson of Spr. & Emeline Eliza Johnson Nostrand
	Dec. 26	Jas. H. Lott of Jamaica & Sarah E. Eldert of Jamaica
1849	Jan. 23	Johannes Lott of Jamaica & Mary Wright, widow of David Jarvis
	--------	Wm. H. Farrington of Spr. & Jane B. Hendrikson of Spr.
	July 18	John Phraner of Jamaica & Mary B. Martin of Jamaica

1849	Aug. 19	Adam Catman & Loisa Wensel
	Aug. 23	Peter s. Nostrand of Flushing & Emma S. Willett of Flushing
	Aug. 24	Wm. Brown of Westchester & Cath. Ann Soper of Jamaica
	Aug. 30	David Schuyler Reeve of Jamaica & Jane Stoothof of Jamaica
	July 19	Garret Bergen of Flatlands & Cath. Jan Bergen of Flatbush
	Oct. 17	Abm. Remsen of New Lots & Sarah Denton of New Lots
	Dec. 26	Cors. Amberson of Jamaica & Eliz. Jane Covert
	Dec. 30	John Soper of Jamaica & Martha Ann Searles of N. T.
1850	Jan. 9	Jacob Bennet of Bushwick & Aletta Ann Allen of Jamaica
	"	Peter Debevoise of N. T. & Margaret Stoothoff of Jamaica
	Feb. 8	John Korness of Flushing & Mary Stark

1850	Feb. 14	Wm. T. Loudon of F. M. & Amelia Nostrand
	Nov. 20	Wm. Nostrand of Spr. & Sarah Ann Amerman of Jamaica
	Nov. 25	Isaac A. Hendickson of Spr. & Cath. Bergen of Jamaica
	April 3	Lawrence Martin, Jr. of Brooklyn & Cath. E. Pittman of Brooklyn
	April 4	Dominicus V. deVeer of Jamaica & Cataline Durye of Jamaica South
	May 19	Robt. Wm. Gordon of East Brooklyn & Margaret Swivilin of Brooklyn
	June 19	John C. Smith of Flushing & Eliz. Nostrand of F. M.
	Sep.---	Wm. Henderson of Jamaica & Eliz. Perry of Jamaica
	Oct. 16	Rich. Spragg of N. T. & Sarah Eliz. V. Wicklen of Jamaica
	Oct. 29	Thos. F. Jenkins of Jamaica & Ann M. Chamberlain of Jamaica
	Dec. 18	Danl. B. Hendickson of Jamaica & Mary Granger of Brooklyn

1850	Dec. 18	Jno. R. Snedeker, ½ way house & Margaret Emmons of Kings Co.
	"	Alfert Henry Dickson & Eliz. Snedeker of Kings Co.
	Dec. 24	Wm. Hendickson of Spr. & Ellen Ann Powell of Jamaica
	"	Jeremiah V. de verg of Flushing & Jane Snedeker of Flushing
	Dec. 29	Nathl. Nostrand of Jamaica & Cath. Sutphin of Jamaica
	Dec. 31	Abm. Stoothof of Jamaica & Phebe Maria Amerman of Jamaica (Rockaway Turnpike)
1851	Feb. 5	Thos. Farrington of Spr. & Phebe Ann Golder of Spr.

A

B

Bishop	51	Buffit	44
Blake	15	Burroughs	1
Bloom	9, 10, 16	Burtis	17, 42
Bliss	19	Byrd	33
Boerum	1, 2, 6, 15, 21		
Bogart	25		

C

Carman	31	Conklin	18, 23, 33, 41, 44
Carmen	37	Cornell	11, 12, 16, 18, 21,
Card	35		24, 25, 28, 39, 43,
Carll	35, 44		44, 46, 48
Carpenter	7, 23, 25, 27, 29, 36, 46	Cornish	12, 14
Case	24	Cornwell	40, 43
Cashaw	23	Cortelyou	4, 11, 25, 34
Cassedy	7	Courten	46
Catman	53	Couwnehoven	5, 10, 11, 12
Chamberlain	4	{Cozine /	4, 6, 10
Chardavoyne	11	Cozyn /	13, 18, 19
Cheshire	49	Cozyne}	24, 49
Chichester	18	Craig	12
Child	3	Crane	41
Coe	5, 11, 17	Creed	12, 25, 40, 44, 50
{Coevert /	9, 11, 17, 24, 38, 53	Cummings	38
Covert}		Curr	32
Coles	16, 23, 31, 41	Curtis	47
Colyer	15, 19, 20, 23, 24, 25, 31		

D

Davison	17	Dodge	20
{Debevois /	1, 6, 7, 8, 10, 11, 13	Doremus	46
Debevoise}	16, 20, 33, 50, 53	Dorland	22, 29, 36, 44
Debois	1	Dorlant	24
Decker	20	Doughty	3, 12
Deeman	9	Douglas	46

E

F

G

Gardner	3	Gorman	38
Garretson	40	Gorsline	16, 27
Gessner	15	Granger	54
Gibson	28	Grater	52
Gildersleeve	15	Gray	13
Godkin	51	Greene	39
Golder	12, 14, 19, 21, 22, 25	Griffin	22, 26, 28, 29
	26, 36, 55	Guthrie	13
Gordon	54		

H

Hall	3	Hewlett	26
Hallet	50	Heyer	29
Hallock	25	Hicks	8, 12, 17, 19,
Ham	38		20, 30, 41
Hammond	34	Higbie	2, 7, 9, 19, 38, 43
Hankison	26	Higgins	4
Hanson	10	Hincksman	16
Hardenbergh	19	Hipwell	34
Harris	36	Hitchcock	50
Hartwell	30	Hoffman	5
Hatfield	16	Hoit	2, 10
Haviland	9	Holland	7, 10
Hegeman	1, 4, 6, 8, 16, 43, 49	Holmes	7, 10, 21
Henderson	17, 45, 47, 48	Hoogland	8, 17, 23
Hendricks	24	Howard	4, 8, 18
{Hendrickson /	1, 2, 7, 8, 9, 13, 16, 18	Howe	32, 37
Hendrkson	19, 22, 23, 24, 25, 26,	Hoyt	31
Hendikson	27, 28, 29, 30, 31, 33,	Hubbs	42, 47
Hendriksen}	34, 36, 37, 38, 39, 44,	Hudson	11
	45, 47, 48, 49, 52,	Hull	51
	54, 55	Hunter	19, 33
Hepburn	11	Hyatt	6, 27, 48
Herriman	8, 45		

M

N

O

P

R

S

T

Terhune	6	Totten	8, 27, 51
Texido	32	Tower	21
Thatford	25	Townsend	7
Thompson	14	Tredwell	41
Thorn (e)	49, 50	Trofford	3
Thornton	17	Turnbull	20
Tilton	5, 40	Turner	17
Titus	14, 19, 34	Tuthill	13, 41
{Tomkins /	3, 6, 14, 47	Tyler	45
Tompkins}		Tyson	40

U

Underhill	5

V

Vail	14	Van Lew	4, 21, 32, 36, 47, 48
Valentine	19, 20, 35, 44, 46, 50	Van Nostrand	12, 22, 39, 42, 46
Van Alst	3, 14, 23, 33, 34		
Van Arsdale	7	Van Nuys	40
Van Arsdalen	20	Van Pelt	15, 19, 29
Van Brunt	11, 13, 16, 31, 35	Van Sicklen	17, 24, 43
Van Buren	13	Van Siclen	26, 31, 32
Van Cott	42	Van Sinderen	19
Van derbrough	11	Van Vleck	39
Van derburgh	14	Van Wi(c)klen	4, 5, 9, 17, 31
Vanderveer	17, 40		37. 38. 48. 50. 54
Vandeveer	8, 19, 21, 54	Van Zandt	23
Vanderverg	55	Van Zant	35
Van Dine	4, 5, 8, 21, 40, 42 44, 51	Vassar	13, 47
Van Dyke	12		
Van Horn	26		

W

Y

Z